Name	Memories and Comments

Name	Memories and Comments

Name	Memories and Comments

Name	Memories and Comments

Name

Memories and Comments

Name

Memories and Comments

Name

Memories and Comments

Name

Memories and Comments

Name	Memories and Comments

Name

Memories and Comments

Name

Memories and Comments

Name

Memories and Comments

Name

Memories and Comments

Name

Memories and Comments

Name

Memories and Comments

Name

Memories and Comments

Name

Memories and Comments

Name

Memories and Comments

Name

Memories and Comments

Name

Memories and Comments

Name

Memories and Comments

Name	Memories and Comments

Name	Memories and Comments

Name	Memories and Comments

Name	Memories and Comments

Name	Memories and Comments

Name	Memories and Comments

Name	Memories and Comments

Name	Memories and Comments

Name	Memories and Comments

Name	Memories and Comments

Name	Memories and Comments

Name	Memories and Comments

Name	Memories and Comments

Name	Memories and Comments

Name	Memories and Comments

Name	Memories and Comments

Name	Memories and Comments

Name	Memories and Comments

Name	Memories and Comments
Name	Memories and Comments
Name	Memories and Comments
Name	Memories and Comments

Name	Memories and Comments

Name	Memories and Comments

Name	Memories and Comments

Name	Memories and Comments

Name	Memories and Comments
Name	Memories and Comments
Name	Memories and Comments
Name	Memories and Comments

Name | Memories and Comments

Name | Memories and Comments

Name | Memories and Comments

Name | Memories and Comments

Name	Memories and Comments

Name	Memories and Comments

Name	Memories and Comments

Name	Memories and Comments

Name

Memories and Comments

Name

Memories and Comments

Name

Memories and Comments

Name

Memories and Comments

Name	Memories and Comments
Name	Memories and Comments
Name	Memories and Comments
Name	Memories and Comments

Name   Memories and Comments

Name   Memories and Comments

Name   Memories and Comments

Name   Memories and Comments

Name	Memories and Comments
Name	Memories and Comments
Name	Memories and Comments
Name	Memories and Comments

Name   **Memories and Comments**

Name   **Memories and Comments**

Name   **Memories and Comments**

Name   **Memories and Comments**

Name	Memories and Comments

Name

Memories and Comments

Name

Memories and Comments

Name

Memories and Comments

Name

Memories and Comments

Name	Memories and Comments

Name	Memories and Comments

Name	Memories and Comments

Name	Memories and Comments

Name

Memories and Comments

Name

Memories and Comments

Name

Memories and Comments

Name

Memories and Comments

Name	Memories and Comments

Name	Memories and Comments

Name	Memories and Comments

Name	Memories and Comments

Name   Memories and Comments

Name   Memories and Comments

Name   Memories and Comments

Name   Memories and Comments

Name	Memories and Comments
Name	Memories and Comments
Name	Memories and Comments
Name	Memories and Comments

Name   *Memories and Comments*

Name   *Memories and Comments*

Name   *Memories and Comments*

Name   *Memories and Comments*

Name

Memories and Comments

Name

Memories and Comments

Name

Memories and Comments

Name

Memories and Comments

Name	Memories and Comments

Name	Memories and Comments

Name	Memories and Comments

Name	Memories and Comments

Name	Memories and Comments
Name	Memories and Comments
Name	Memories and Comments
Name	Memories and Comments

Name

Memories and Comments

Name

Memories and Comments

Name

Memories and Comments

Name

Memories and Comments

Name	Memories and Comments

Name

Memories and Comments

Name

Memories and Comments

Name

Memories and Comments

Name

Memories and Comments

Name

Memories and Comments

Name

Memories and Comments

Name

Memories and Comments

Name

Memories and Comments

Name

Memories and Comments

Name

Memories and Comments

Name

Memories and Comments

Name

Memories and Comments

Name	Memories and Comments

Name	Memories and Comments

Name	Memories and Comments

Name	Memories and Comments

Name

Memories and Comments

Name

Memories and Comments

Name

Memories and Comments

Name

Memories and Comments

Name

Memories and Comments

Name

Memories and Comments

Name

Memories and Comments

Name

Memories and Comments

Name

Memories and Comments

Name

Memories and Comments

Name

Memories and Comments

Name

Memories and Comments

Name   Memories and Comments

Name   Memories and Comments

Name   Memories and Comments

Name   Memories and Comments

Name

Memories and Comments

Name

Memories and Comments

Name

Memories and Comments

Name

Memories and Comments

Name

Memories and Comments

Name

Memories and Comments

Name

Memories and Comments

Name

Memories and Comments

Name

Memories and Comments

Name

Memories and Comments

Name

Memories and Comments

Name

Memories and Comments

Name	Memories and Comments

Name	Memories and Comments

Name	Memories and Comments

Name	Memories and Comments

Name	Memories and Comments

Name	Memories and Comments
Name	Memories and Comments
Name	Memories and Comments
Name	Memories and Comments

Name

Memories and Comments

Name

Memories and Comments

Name

Memories and Comments

Name

Memories and Comments

Name	Memories and Comments

Name	Memories and Comments

Name	Memories and Comments

Name	Memories and Comments

Name

Memories and Comments

Name

Memories and Comments

Name

Memories and Comments

Name

Memories and Comments

Name

Memories and Comments

Name

Memories and Comments

Name

Memories and Comments

Name

Memories and Comments

Name   *Memories and Comments*

Name   *Memories and Comments*

Name   *Memories and Comments*

Name   *Memories and Comments*

Name	Memories and Comments

Name	Memories and Comments

Name	Memories and Comments

Name	Memories and Comments

Name	Memories and Comments

Name	Memories and Comments

Name	Memories and Comments

Name	Memories and Comments

Name   Memories and Comments

Name   Memories and Comments

Name   Memories and Comments

Name   Memories and Comments

Name   Memories and Comments

Name   Memories and Comments

Name   Memories and Comments

Name   Memories and Comments

Name

Memories and Comments

Name

Memories and Comments

Name

Memories and Comments

Name

Memories and Comments

Name

Memories and Comments

Name

Memories and Comments

Name

Memories and Comments

Name

Memories and Comments

Name

Memories and Comments

Name

Memories and Comments

Name

Memories and Comments

Name

Memories and Comments

Name	Memories and Comments

Name	Memories and Comments

Name	Memories and Comments

Name	Memories and Comments

Name	Memories and Comments
Name	Memories and Comments
Name	Memories and Comments
Name	Memories and Comments

Name   Memories and Comments

Name   Memories and Comments

Name   Memories and Comments

Name   Memories and Comments

Name

Memories and Comments

Name

Memories and Comments

Name

Memories and Comments

Name

Memories and Comments

Name	Memories and Comments

Name	Memories and Comments

Name	Memories and Comments

Name	Memories and Comments

Name	Memories and Comments

Name	Memories and Comments

Name	Memories and Comments

Name	Memories and Comments

Name   Memories and Comments

Name   Memories and Comments

Name   Memories and Comments

Name   Memories and Comments